The New Colossus

EMMA LAZARUS

Not like the brazen giant of Greek fame,
With conquering limbs astride from land to land;
Here at our sea-washed, sunset gates shall stand
A mighty woman with a torch, whose flame
Is the imprisoned lightning, and her name
Mother of Exiles. From her beacon-hand
Glows world-wide welcome; her mild eyes command
The air-bridged harbor that twin cities frame.
"Keep, ancient lands, your storied pomp!" cries she
With silent lips. "Give me your tired, your poor,
Your huddled masses yearning to breathe free,
The wretched refuse of your teeming shore.
Send these, the homeless, tempest-tost to me.
I lift my lamp beside the golden door!"

— Emma Lazarus

GATEWAY TO FREEDOM

The Story of
the Statue of Liberty
and Ellis Island

JIM HARGROVE

CHILDRENS PRESS ®

CHICAGO

PICTURE ACKNOWLEDGMENTS

© 1986 Peter B. Kaplan—Front cover, 2, 5, 8 (right), 11, 13, 17, 100 (right); 107 (left), 108 (top right, bottom), 110, 111; © 1984: 24, 62 (left), 96, 100 (left), 103, 104, 105 (right), 106 (top and bottom left); © 1982: 25 (right), 99 (top and bottom right)

© H. Armstrong Roberts, Inc.—1 (top), 20 (bottom right)

Historical Pictures Service, Chicago—1 (bottom), 10 (right), 20 (top), 23, 40, 42, 51, 53, 58, 63

AP/Wide World—6, 12, 20 (bottom left), 72, 81, 82, 94, 105 (left), 106 (right), 107 (right), 108 (top left)

© Photri—8 (left), 18, 29, 41, 43, 46 (bottom), 64, 69, 71, 73 (top), 74, 75, 79, 85, 86, 99 (left)

© Roloc Color Slides—9, 27 (top), 59, 76, 83, 90, 95, back cover

Nawrocki Stock Photo—© Wm. S. Nawrocki: 10 (left)

Journalism Services—© Rick Maiman: 15, 25 (left), 31 (right), 109

© EKM-Nepenthe—22, 67, 70

New-York Historical Society—27 (bottom left and right), 28, 32, 55

National Park Service—31 (left), 62 (right), 73 (bottom), 78, 84, 88, 89, 93

Museum of the City of New York—34, 36, 37, 39, 52, 56, 61, 80

New York Public Library—45, 46 (top), 47, 48, 49

Editor: Shari Joffe
Design: Karen A. Yops

Library of Congress Cataloging-in-Publication Data

Hargrove, Jim.
  Gateway to freedom: the story of the Statue of
Liberty and Ellis Island.

  Includes index.
  Summary: Describes the designing of the giant statue in
New York Harbor, the ideals of enlightenment and liberty for
which it stands, and the immigration activities associated with
nearby Ellis Island.
  1. Statue of Liberty (New York, N.Y.)—Juvenile
literature. 2. Statue of Liberty National Monument (New
York, N.Y.)—Juvenile literature. 3. Ellis Island
Immigration Station (New York, N.Y.)—Juvenile literature.
4. United States—Emigration and immigration—Juvenile
literature. 5. New York (N.Y.)—Buildings, structures,
etc.—Juvenile literature. [1. Statue of Liberty (New York,
N.Y.) 2. Ellis Island Immigration Station (New York,
N.Y.) 3. United States—Emigration and immigration.
4. National monuments. 5. Statues] I. Title.
F128.64.L6H34   1986   974.7'1   86-14707
ISBN 0-516-03296-8

Chapter 1

The Torch of Freedom

For a century, she has stood in New York Harbor like a proud and kindly giant, a symbol of freedom for generations of Americans. For millions of immigrants who first traveled to America's shores in ships passing through her shadow, she has symbolized hope. To the French sculptor who created her, she was *Liberty Enlightening the World.* The rest of us know her simply as the Statue of Liberty.

The year 1986 marked the hundredth anniversary of America's largest and best-known national symbol. In the months and years leading up to July 4, 1986, Americans planned for an enormous birthday celebration. Many millions of dollars were collected so that Liberty could be cleaned and repaired in time for her party.

The Statue of Liberty and the island on which she stands are part of the national park system. In addition to being an important symbol, the Statue of Liberty is one of the most popular tourist attractions in the United States. About 1.7 million people visit the great statue every year.

A tall ship parades by the Statue of Liberty during Liberty Weekend '86, America's four-day celebration of the statue's hundredth anniversary.

Although millions have traveled to see the statue, making it all the way to the top of her crown is no easy task. To get there, most visitors first ride on a ferryboat that travels the short distance from Manhattan to Liberty Island. An elevator carries tourists to the top of Liberty's stone and concrete pedestal.

When the elevator reaches its highest point, it has only arrived at the statue's feet. From the top of the pedestal, a spiral staircase winds up, and up, and up—171 steps—to Liberty's crown. Reaching her crown is like climbing to the top of a fifteen-story building. It is an unusual and tiring experience. The outside of the Statue of Liberty has an elegant simplicity. The inside is more like a fantastic dream. While climbing the seemingly endless stairs, it is easy to forget how Liberty looks from the outside. The interior view is unlike anything most people have ever seen.

Visitors can reach Liberty's crown by climbing a spiral staircase inside the statue.

Liberty's "skin," the part of the statue visible from the outside, is made of extremely thin copper. It is less than one-tenth of an inch thick. The statue is held up by an incredible network of thousands of iron girders. From the inside, the girders reach out toward Liberty's thin outer skin from every possible angle. On the way up the long staircase, a person can see nearly all the thousands of iron supports.

When visitors arrive at the crown, they have reached the end of their long journey. Inside the crown is an observation room that can hold about twenty people. For the first time since beginning their long climb, visitors can look down on New York and its harbor. A series of windows almost surrounds the observation room.

F.A. Bartholdi, Statue of Liberty Sculptor

The Statue of Liberty was designed by French sculptor Frédéric Auguste Bartholdi (left). American architect Richard Morris Hunt (right) designed the statue's pedestal.

The view from the top is spectacular. Manhattan, Brooklyn, the Hudson and East rivers, the Atlantic Ocean, Upper New York Bay, and portions of New Jersey are all visible from Liberty's crown. But it is not the grand view alone that brings so many people to the statue each year. For the majority of visitors, Liberty has a meaning all her own.

A SYMBOL OF AMERICA

The Statue of Liberty was designed more than a hundred years ago by French sculptor Frédéric Auguste Bartholdi. Bartholdi designed all the parts of the statue that are visible from the outside. The complicated iron support system was created by another Frenchman, Gustave Eiffel, who some years later designed the famous Eiffel Tower in Paris. An American architect named Richard Morris Hunt designed Liberty's pedestal.

When the statue was unveiled in 1886, it was the tallest man-made structure in the world. The highest point of the great

structure is the torch, which towers 305 feet above the base. In art and literature of the past, a flaming torch has had several meanings. In some works of art, torches were carried by soldiers fighting for a revolutionary cause. In others, the torch was a symbol of enlightenment. Bartholdi intended Liberty's torch to provide a beacon of light cutting through the darkness: a symbol of the power of truth and freedom.

The tablet held in Liberty's left hand represents the law and bears the date of the Declaration of Independence.

On Liberty's head, Bartholdi placed a crown with seven spikes. The spikes symbolized rays of the sun sending light to the seven planets that, in Bartholdi's time, were known to revolve around it. (The eighth and ninth planets, Neptune and Pluto, were not discovered until later.) The seven rays of Liberty's crown also brought the "light of liberty" to the seven continents and seven seas of the world. The statue's left hand holds a stone tablet with the inscription JULY IV MDCCLXXVI. The Roman numerals stand for July 4, 1776, the famous date of America's Declaration of Independence from England.

One of the statue's most powerful symbols is not even visible in most photographs. A length of broken chain lies at Liberty's feet. Bartholdi intended this to be a reminder that the United States was still a relatively young republic. When the statue was erected, America had been free of England's tyranny for only a hundred years. With her chains newly broken, Liberty stands proudly, a symbol of freedom for all the world to see.

That the great statue represented the ideals of enlightenment, truth, and liberty is clear from the symbols Bartholdi included within it. But from almost the moment the statue was assembled in New York Harbor, it began to take on another meaning as well — one that may also have been part of Bartholdi's plan.

The broken chain at Liberty's feet was meant to symbolize America's newly won independence from England.

13

The Statue of Liberty stands about a mile southwest of the southern tip of Manhattan Island and about thirteen hundred feet from the New Jersey shore. But Liberty faces neither New York nor New Jersey. Instead, she looks directly toward the open water of New York Harbor. The best view of her is from ships moving northward from the Atlantic toward Upper New York Bay. At first, it may seem strange that Bartholdi placed his statue facing the sea. Toward whom was she looking?

IN LIBERTY'S SHADOW

About one-half mile north of Liberty Island is another small island. Though it is now visited only by tourists, this little plot of dry land near the New Jersey shore was once the destination of one of the largest human migrations the world has ever seen. Over a period of about half a century, between twelve and sixteen million people from all over the world came to the little island. On Ellis Island, as it was called, immigrants seeking a new home in America were examined by officials of the United States government. The officials determined which newcomers would be permitted to enter the United States.

It has been many decades since Ellis Island was used as an immigration center. Over the years, its buildings have decayed and fallen into disrepair. Recently, as part of the Statue of Liberty-Ellis Island centennial celebration preparations, workers have begun to restore the buildings to their original state.

Today, a visitor to the nearly deserted island might find it hard to imagine how crowded it once was. During the early years of the twentieth century, armies of bewildered immigrants were brought to Ellis Island after being carried across the Atlantic Ocean in huge ships. There, often with the help of interpreters, they would answer long lists of questions to determine whether or not they were fit to enter the United States.

For most immigrants, New York Harbor marked the end of a long and difficult journey. In that busy harbor, the full meaning of the Statue of Liberty became clear. The great statue did not face the New Jersey shore, the part of the mainland nearest her. Nor did Liberty face Manhattan Island, the teeming center of New York City. Instead, she looked directly over the waters of the harbor, squarely facing the immigrant travelers who, at last, had arrived in America.

For millions of immigrants, Liberty symbolized hope — hope that a new and better way of life could be found in America.

REKINDLING THE FLAME

During the last years of the nineteenth century and the first few decades of the twentieth, the Statue of Liberty and Ellis Island

Ellis Island, which is located about one-half mile north of the Statue of Liberty, was the entranceway to America for more than twelve million immigrants from all over the world.

were twin features in the dreams of millions of immigrants. Liberty symbolized hope and freedom in America; Ellis Island provided the reality. But as the years passed, both the statue and the activities on Ellis Island began to change.

As early as 1886, the year the Statue of Liberty was unveiled, many Americans were beginning to feel that some restrictions had to be placed on immigration to the United States. By the 1920s, laws had been passed that severely limited the number of people who could move to the United States. By the years of World War II, the huge immigration center at Ellis Island was no longer needed to process the diminishing number of immigrants seeking entry into America through New York Harbor. In 1954, the island was abandoned, and its buildings were allowed to crumble.

As the years went by, the saltwater, winds, and pollution of New York Harbor took their toll on the Statue of Liberty as well. Even by 1911, Liberty's twenty-fifth anniversary, some problems had been discovered. "Already the metal is eaten through in some places, and an examination from the interior of the statue shows about fifty or seventy-five small holes in the gown," reported the July 24, 1911, edition of the *New York Times*. "These holes vary in size from pinpoints to openings as large as a quarter of a dollar," the story continued. "All show ragged edges where the work of corrosion is still going on."

Small repairs were made on the statue at various times during the 1900s, but by the 1970s it was clear that a greater effort was needed. The torch was leaking and in serious disrepair. Small chunks of it actually had fallen to the ground. The iron supports of the interior, particularly those inside the arm holding the torch, were badly corroded. Some engineers feared that a bad windstorm might cause the arm to fall off. Other improvements were needed as well.

In 1980 and 1981, a group of Frenchmen had a wonderful idea. They suggested that since the Statue of Liberty had originally been a gift from the people of France to the people of America, perhaps France could help the United States repair it. Working with the

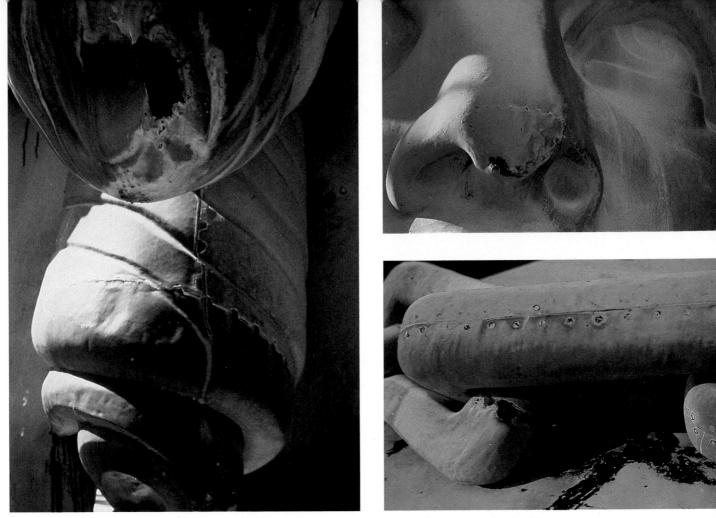

By the 1970s, Liberty was in need of major repairs. In many places, her copper skin had become damaged by years of exposure to saltwater, wind, and pollution. In a few places, such as on one of her curls (left), the copper had been completely eaten away. Many areas were corroded and stained with rust, including the tip of her nose (top right) and the chain near her feet (bottom right).

United States National Park Service, the Frenchmen founded the French-American Committee for Restoration of the Statue of Liberty. Almost at once, French engineers traveled to New York to examine the statue and determine what repairs would be needed.

In May 1982, American President Ronald Reagan announced the creation of another committee to help restore Liberty. But this committee would also raise money to restore the Ellis Island immigration center to its original condition. The committee was called the Statue of Liberty-Ellis Island Centennial Commission. Heading the group was Lee Iacocca, the popular chairman of the Chrysler Corporation. The committee had to face the difficult task

of raising about $230 million from private sources. Of this huge total, about $30 million would be spent to have the Statue of Liberty restored by July 4, 1986. A far larger amount, about $140 million, would be needed to repair the buildings, grounds, and seawall on Ellis Island. It was hoped that this work could be completed by 1992, the hundredth anniversary of the island's opening as an immigration center. The remaining money would be saved for future repairs and administrative costs.

By 1984, it was clear to observers that Liberty was the focus of an extensive restoration project. Huge scaffolds hundreds of feet tall had been built all around the statue. To some people, the sight must have been startling. From a distance, the complex scaffolding looked like the iron bars of a jail cell. It appeared almost as if Liberty had been imprisoned.

The cost of the restoration project tells much about how the world has changed in the last hundred years. When the statue was built in the 1880s, French citizens donated about $400,000 to pay for the cost of just the statue itself. Americans donated about $300,000 to build the pedestal and erect the statue. By 1886, the total cost of building and mounting the statue was about $700,000. A century later, it would cost more than forty times that much, about $30 million, just to clean and repair it.

"With care and looking after," Bartholdi had claimed, "the monument will last as long as those built by the Egyptians." Americans clearly hope that it will. But the great statue, like the ideal she stands for, obviously needs our constant care.

The scaffolding constructed during restoration of the statue is thought to be the largest ever built. It was designed to move no more than three inches in a 100-mile-an-hour wind, and was separated from the skin by eighteen inches at all points to avoid damage to the statue.

Chapter 2

In Old New York Harbor

Before European explorers reached the New World, the islands in and around New York Bay were often visited by Mohegan and Manhattan Indians. The Mohegans referred to tiny Ellis Island as *Kilshk*, or Gull Island, because sea gulls flocked there to feed on the oysters that were plentiful near its shores. Historians believe that Ellis Island, and perhaps Liberty Island as well, once served as favorite Indian fishing spots.

In 1609, English explorer Henry Hudson and a crew hired by the Dutch East India Company sailed into New York Bay aboard the *Half Moon*. Before heading up the wide river that now bears his name, Hudson claimed for the Dutch the land—and the islands— that he saw. He was not the first European explorer to enter the bay of New York. Some eighty-five years earlier, in 1524, Italian explorer Giovanni da Verrazano had sighted Manhattan Island while exploring the northeastern coast of the United States. It was the Dutch, however, who laid claim to the area.

By 1625, the Dutch had established a trading post and small settlement called New Amsterdam on the southern tip of Manhattan. After buying the island from the Indians with a few

English explorer Henry Hudson (bottom left) sailed into New York Bay in 1609 (bottom right) and claimed Manhattan Island and the islands surrounding it for the Dutch. In 1626, the Dutch formally bought the island from the Indians for about twenty-four dollars' worth of goods (top).

Manhattan Island as it appeared in the mid-1600s, when it was a thriving Dutch colony called New Amsterdam

dollars' worth of trinkets, they developed New Amsterdam into a thriving little colony.

The Dutch bought Ellis Island, which they called Oyster Island, from the Indians in 1634. The first known private owner was a man named Michael Paauw. Although it was privately owned, for many years Oyster Island was a favorite vacation spot for Dutch colonists.

THE ENGLISH TAKE CONTROL

In 1664, King Charles II of England decided to give a huge area of land in the New World, including Manhattan and the smaller islands near it, to his brother James, the duke of York. Since he thought the Dutch colonists might object to the gift, the king sent a fleet of warships to Manhattan and seized control of New Amsterdam. In honor of his brother, the English king renamed the colony New York.

The two tiny islands in the bay now came under English rule. Only three years after the English conquest, the little plot of dry land now called Liberty Island came under the ownership of a man named Isaac Bedloe. For many years, including the first seventy years it was home to the Statue of Liberty, the island was known as Bedloe's Island. The name Liberty Island was not adopted until 1956. At various times during the 1700s, Bedloe's Island was used as a hospital for people with serious infectious diseases such as smallpox.

Manhattan Island in 1673, nine years after the English seized control of New Amsterdam and the islands surrounding it

Around the time of the American Revolution, the land now called Ellis Island was used as a place to execute a number of notorious pirates. The first man executed there was a pirate named Anderson, in 1765. A few months earlier, while leading a shipboard mutiny, Anderson had murdered every member of his ship's crew except one little boy. He was captured after he forced the boy to row him to a nearby island.

AFTER THE AMERICAN REVOLUTION

During the early years of the revolutionary war, Bedloe's Island became a sanctuary for Tories (those who wanted America to remain under British rule). The little island was often raided by American patriots.

When the American Revolution ended in 1783, possession of the two islands in Upper New York Bay changed for the last time. In little more than 150 years, control of the islands had passed from the Indians to the Dutch, to the English, and finally to the Americans. Before long, the young government would go to extraordinary lengths to protect the two islands.

In 1785, a man named Samuel Ellis offered for sale the plot of land known as Oyster Island. No record exists to show how he came to own it. But ever since that time, the island has been known as Ellis Island. Samuel Ellis was not able to sell the island, and it remained in his family until it was purchased, some years later, by the state of New York.

At the end of the eighteenth century, Emperor Napoleon Bonaparte of France began a series of wars that would last for nearly twenty years. Many Americans were fearful that the United States would be drawn into the fighting, which was particularly fierce between France and England. Ellis and Bedloe's islands were ideally situated to defend New York Harbor, as well as the city itself, from attack by sea.

By 1798, a quarter of a million dollars in funds from the federal and New York State governments had been used to build up defenses in New York Harbor. A fort with barracks large enough to hold a company of soldiers was completed on Ellis Island the same year. Two years later, the state of New York gave Bedloe's Island and a portion of Ellis Island to the federal government so that better fortifications could be built. Over the next few years, more than a million dollars was spent on fortifications in and around New York Harbor. In 1808, the federal government paid ten thousand dollars to become the owner of the remaining property on Ellis Island.

Many taxpayers complained that this was too high a price for such a tiny island. Sometimes, when the water of New York Harbor was at high tide, the low-lying island was almost covered by water. Nevertheless, most people realized that the island could provide a valuable base from which to defend New York City against attack.

Before the War of 1812 began, important forts were built on both Ellis and Bedloe's islands. Little remains of Fort Gibson, the fortress on Ellis Island that housed as many as 180 American troops during the War of 1812. But Fort Wood, built between 1808 and 1811 on Bedloe's Island, is of great importance to anyone interested in the Statue of Liberty. The fort's thick walls were built in the shape of an eleven-point star. Although Fort Wood never saw a battle and fell into disrepair by the 1870s, its star-shaped walls were eventually repaired to help form the foundation for the great statue's pedestal. These walls can be seen today by anyone who visits the Statue of Liberty.

During the War of 1812 and again during the Civil War, Ellis and Bedloe's islands were used as troop stations. After the Civil

The star-shaped walls of Fort Wood, which had been built on Bedloe's Island in the early 1800s to help defend New York against naval attack, were used to form the foundation for the statue's pedestal.

War ended in 1865, many residents of New York and New Jersey were shocked to learn that huge and dangerous stores of explosive gunpowder and other munitions were being stored on both islands. A number of newspapers reported that if the ammunition dumps were accidentally ignited, they would create explosions large enough to threaten much of New York City and the New Jersey shore. Despite public outcry, the explosives were allowed to remain on the islands for some time. The public had ample reason for concern. In the twentieth century, several explosions near Ellis Island would cause serious damage as far as a mile and a half away in downtown Manhattan. But even by the 1870s, there was a growing public awareness that New York Harbor was becoming a dangerous place. New Yorkers, and Americans in general, were becoming alarmed about another issue as well.

ARMIES OF IMMIGRANTS

Since the earliest days of colonization, America has been a land of immigrants. The continual westward expansion of the United States seemed always to make room for new immigrants from the Old World. During America's early years, the waves of weary travelers were mostly English, Dutch, French, Scotch-Irish, and German. By the middle of the nineteenth century, new immigrant groups began crossing the Atlantic. These travelers included Italians, Irish, Austrians, Scandinavians, Jews, and eastern Europeans.

Much of America's strength had come from the diversity of the settlers in the new land. But soon after the end of the Civil War, many Americans began to worry about their nation's "open-door" immigration policy. Some Americans were prejudiced against the people from southern and eastern Europe, whose cultures were vastly different from their own. Rumors, some printed in magazines and newspapers, told of European nations emptying their prisons, mental institutions, and poorhouses, and sending the inmates to America.

Opposite Page: A pair of 1854 lithographs show the transformation of a poor Irishman bound for New York (bottom left) into a well-dressed gentleman ready to return to his homeland after having found fortune in America (bottom right). An 1871 cartoon (top), which shows Uncle Sam welcoming a motley assortment of immigrants, expressed the growing desire of many Americans to restrict immigration to the United States.

The eight million immigrants who arrived in New York between 1855 and 1890 were processed through Castle Garden, an old fort at the southern tip of Manhattan.

Americans began to worry about the immigrants who streamed into New York Harbor. The immigrants, on the other hand, had plenty of reasons to worry about their new home in America. Throughout the eighteenth and most of the nineteenth centuries, the United States had no nationwide immigration policy. Individual states were permitted to make up their own rules. Immigrants arriving in America faced a great many dangers, and few government agencies seemed able to protect them.

In the years before Ellis Island became an immigration center, most immigrants who arrived at New York Harbor were sent to an old fort in southern Manhattan called Castle Garden. Despite frequent investigations by the New York State government, many abuses in and around Castle Garden went unchecked.

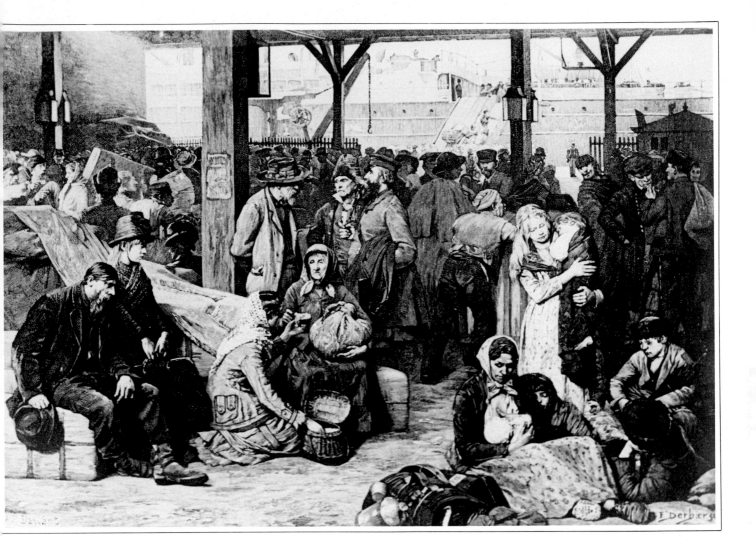

Many of the vulnerable immigrants had their entire savings stolen from them or were cheated by the people who changed their foreign currency into American dollars. Some unscrupulous railroad agents sent immigrants to faraway areas of the country, just to make more money from ticket sales. A few unlucky travelers were even kidnapped and forced to work on railroads and other labor projects.

Eventually, the new immigration center on Ellis Island would put an end to much of the injustice suffered by those arriving in New York. But before this occurred, a visitor from France would do much to change the image of New York Harbor. In the meantime, disregarding the many dangers, immigrants continued to travel to America by the hundreds of thousands.

Because there was no federal regulation of immigration throughout most of the 1800s, abuses occurred frequently at Castle Garden. The facilities were unsanitary and overcrowded, and immigrants were often treated unfairly. Public outrage finally forced the center's closing in 1890.

THE VISITOR FROM FRANCE

On June 21, 1871, the French steamer *Pereire* sailed into the crowded waters off the southern tip of Manhattan. The busiest port in the Western Hemisphere, New York Harbor was alive with ships of almost every description. Tiny rowboats and dinghies were carefully steered away from the giant sailing ships heading in and out of the port. Great steamships such as the *Pereire* were only beginning to replace the slower sailing vessels. The power of steam had enabled the *Pereire* to cross the Atlantic Ocean in only thirteen days. A few decades earlier, before the advent of steamships, a voyage across the Atlantic took a month or more.

Some of the passengers aboard the *Pereire* were immigrants seeking a new home in America. One of the passengers, a thirty-seven-year-old French sculptor, was merely a visitor. Frédéric Auguste Bartholdi had sailed to America in order to learn more about its land and people. For some time, the sculptor had been thinking about a grand idea. Bartholdi planned to design an enormous statue, perhaps the largest in the world, that would be paid for by the people of France and given to the people of the United States as a token of friendship.

It was an idea that Bartholdi and other French people had been considering for about five years. Bartholdi was the friend of a distinguished French writer and teacher named Édouard René Lefebvre de Laboulaye. Like Bartholdi, Professor Laboulaye was intensely interested in the United States. He had even written a number of books about America.

At a dinner party at Laboulaye's house in 1865, the professor, Bartholdi, and other guests began talking about the friendship between France and the United States. Laboulaye suggested that a monument to independence be built in the United States to memorialize the long-standing alliance between the two countries. France had helped the United States in its struggle for independence from England. As America's ally during the revolutionary war, France had provided large-scale military aid, including an army and a powerful fleet. Considering the

French scholar Édouard de Laboulaye (left) was the person who first suggested to Bartholdi that a monument to American independence be built in America by the French. Bartholdi expressed the long-standing friendship between the two countries in his sculpture of Lafayette and Washington (right), which now stands in New York City. Lafayette was a French statesman who fought for American independence during the revolutionary war.

relationship between France and America, the professor suggested that the monument be "built by united effort, [as] if it were a common work of both nations."

A number of other people at Laboulaye's party were also interested in the project. Several would eventually contribute money to help Bartholdi construct the Statue of Liberty. But it would be years before the undertaking would go much beyond the planning stages.

Part of the delay was caused by the unstable political situation in France at the time. France was at war with Germany between 1870 and 1871. Bartholdi himself had to fight in this war. Also, France

This is the way New York Harbor looked when Bartholdi first visited the United States in 1871. Bedloe's Island, the site Bartholdi chose for the Statue of Liberty, is the tiny island above circular Castle Garden. Ellis Island is the larger island on the left.

was not a democracy, but was ruled with an iron hand by Emperor Napoleon III. Some French citizens might have feared that a great statue symbolizing liberty would be frowned on by the government. But Bartholdi did not look at it that way.

A prominent statue in America dedicated to the ideal of freedom, Bartholdi thought, might inspire French people to desire greater liberty as well. In a letter to his friend Professor Laboulaye, Bartholdi wrote, "I will try to glorify the Republic and Liberty over there, in the hope that someday I will find it again here."

Bartholdi began to think he had found a place for his statue soon after the *Pereire* steamed into New York Harbor. Bedloe's Island seemed like the ideal spot. From there, his huge statue would greet thousands of immigrants every year as their ships sailed into the busy port. A great deal of work had to be done, however, before the sculpture could become a reality. First, Bartholdi would have to convince the Americans to provide the land and a base for the statue. Then he would have to convince his French countrymen to help pay for building it. Only then could the work begin in earnest.

Bartholdi used his five-month-long trip to America to good advantage. With letters of introduction from Laboulaye, whose books were well known in America, he was able to meet many important Americans. Traveling by train from New York to California and back again, he visited such cities as Chicago, San Francisco, Salt Lake City, Denver, St. Louis, and Pittsburgh. He even talked about his grand idea with Ulysses S. Grant at the American president's summer home in New Jersey.

In Massachusetts, he had several visits with American poet Henry Wadsworth Longfellow. In Washington, D. C., Senator Charles Sumner showed him the sights of the capital, including the unfinished Washington Monument, which hadn't been worked on in fifteen years.

Bartholdi made it clear to everyone he met that the French people would pay for the enormous statue he was planning. It would be a gift to America from the people of France. When he returned to France, the sculptor was able to report that everyone in America seemed in favor of the gift. The United States Congress, he was sure, would soon establish Bedloe's Island as the spot for the statue.

But the enthusiasm the Americans felt for Bartholdi's grand idea soon faded. There was much work left to be done, in the United States as well as in France, before the Statue of Liberty could be built.

Fortunately, Bartholdi was satisfied with his first visit to America. Although he was aware that there might be problems ahead, he was convinced that the idea could be made to work. He would build the largest statue ever constructed in modern times, it would be erected on Bedloe's Island in New York Harbor, and it would be called *Liberty Enlightening the World*.

Chapter 3

Liberty Enlightening the World

Bartholdi returned to France in the fall of 1871 filled with enthusiasm for the huge statue he planned to build. But following the defeat of the armies of Napoleon III by Germany, France was in near chaos. No one seemed to agree about what kind of government France should have, and several would rise and fall before Bartholdi began work on the Statue of Liberty.

For the next four years, Bartholdi, Laboulaye, and a few other Frenchmen who championed the plan kept their ideas to themselves. Finally, in 1875, France settled on a constitution that gave some order to its government. At last, a decade after they had conceived of the monument, Bartholdi, Laboulaye, and their friends could begin work on the great project.

In August of 1875, Bartholdi completed a four-foot-tall clay model of the statue, and Laboulaye organized the Union Franco-Americaine (French-American Union) to raise funds to build the enormous statue. The equivalent of about four hundred thousand American dollars would be needed.

Bartholdi was probably not surprised that it took the Union Franco-Americaine six years to collect the necessary funds. The

Workmen building the final plaster model for Liberty's head in Bartholdi's Paris studio

A bronze of Bartholdi's first model for the head of the statue

sculptor had built large statues before (though none as large as this), and he knew that such things took a considerable amount of time. But he was not about to wait until all the money had been raised to begin work.

FIRST STEPS TOWARD LIBERTY

The clay model of Liberty that Bartholdi presented to the Union Franco-Americaine looked very much like the final statue would look. But before he arrived at that final design, Bartholdi produced at least five other clay models. In the earliest miniatures, Liberty carried a torch in her left hand. The torch did not shift to her right hand until the fourth model. Only in the sixth model did the statue wear a star-shaped crown and hold a tablet in her left hand.

In one of Bartholdi's earliest small-scale models of the statue (left), Liberty's left hand is empty. A later model done in 1879 (right) more closely resembles the final statue.

About a decade had passed between the time Professor Laboulaye first suggested the work and the completion by Bartholdi of the first clearly recognizable model. But after 1875, the pace began to quicken. When he was satisfied with the clay model, Bartholdi made a series of increasingly larger plaster models. He used a huge warehouse in Paris as his studio. Before long, the studio was filled with models of Liberty, as well as with other projects the sculptor was working on. But none of the other projects approached the size of the Statue of Liberty. Even the models of Liberty were enormous.

The first plaster model was more than nine feet tall. When Bartholdi was satisfied with it, he made hundreds of careful measurements so that a second plaster model four times as large could be made. The second model was more than thirty-six feet high, but even this was small compared to the final plaster model, which would be the same size as the finished statue. Because no building in Paris was large enough to house such a huge work, Bartholdi built this last model in many separate sections.

Eventually, the sculptor and his assistants would build huge wooden forms that conformed to the exact shape of the plaster model. Then thin sheets of copper would be placed inside each form and hammered into the final shape of Liberty's outer skin. As difficult and expensive as this work would be, there were other problems to be overcome as well.

For a time, Bartholdi and his friends hoped that the statue would be finished by 1876, the hundredth anniversary of America's Declaration of Independence. But it soon became clear that it would be impossible to have the statue ready in time.

A lack of money was one of the reasons for the delay. Bartholdi realized it would be difficult to raise the large amount of money needed to finish such an enormous project. In order to help raise money for the statue itself and for the foundation and pedestal in America, Bartholdi knew he would have to become a bit of a showman.

Although the complete statue existed only as a plaster model, the sculptor managed to finish the torch and a portion of the right arm by 1876. About 900,000 spectators looked on in awe when the thirty-foot-high section was shown in Philadelphia that same year.

Many people found it difficult to believe that the huge arm could be only a small part of an even bigger statue. One finger of Liberty's hand was taller than a man. A single fingernail was more than a foot across. A dozen visitors could stand inside the circular railing of the torch.

Although Bartholdi could not, as he had hoped, finish the entire statue by the American centennial in 1876, he was able to display the torch and a portion of the right arm at the 1876 International Exhibition in Philadelphia. Visitors were charged fifty cents to climb up to the balcony surrounding the torch. The money was used to help finance construction of the rest of the statue.

Some of the people who came to see the amazing attraction were from New York City, where Bartholdi planned to erect the statue. Some of the New Yorkers wondered aloud whether such a colossal statue could ever be built. There was so much skepticism, in fact, that at one point Bartholdi suggested that Liberty might find a friendlier home in Philadelphia.

This suggestion had precisely the effect the sculptor had hoped it would have. Suddenly, New Yorkers realized that they didn't want

French engineer Eugène Emmanuel Viollet-le-Duc, who planned to support the statue with sand-filled compartments, died before his plan could be carried out.

to lose the great statue. The very next year, a New York politician named William M. Evarts organized a committee to raise money to build a foundation and pedestal for the Statue of Liberty. If nothing else, committee members pointed out, the statue could be used as a lighthouse for ships. It would take years to obtain all the money needed for Liberty's pedestal, however. In the meantime, Bartholdi had other problems.

LIBERTY'S SKELETON

The French sculptor realized that Liberty's thin copper skin would not be strong enough to stand up to the terrific winds that often blew across New York Harbor. From the beginning, he knew that some form of interior support would be needed.

To solve the problem, Bartholdi worked with a French engineer named Eugène Emmanuel Viollet-le-Duc. Viollet-le-Duc planned to support the great statue with walled compartments filled with sand. The sand would not only help the statue support its own weight, but would also make it heavy enough to stand up to strong winds. Bartholdi was still planning to use this system when he displayed Liberty's arm in Philadelphia in 1876, and even in 1878,

The head of the statue was exhibited at the 1878 Paris International Fair.

when the great statue's head was shown at the Paris International Fair.

But Viollet-le-Duc died the following year, well before he had finished designing the elaborate system of supports. Suddenly Bartholdi, who was an expert artist but understood little about engineering, was left without a definite plan for supporting the statue.

The man who came to Bartholdi's rescue was Alexandre Gustave Eiffel. Eiffel had become famous throughout France and much of Europe for his spectacular designs for steel bridges. He had

French engineer Alexandre Gustave Eiffel (left) devised an ingenious skeletal support system for the Statue of Liberty (right).

discovered how to link together steel girders so that they would be slightly flexible. The result was that his bridges were strong enough to span great distances, yet had the flexibility to absorb the great shock of heavy, fast-moving objects such as trains.

Soon after the death of Viollet-le-Duc, Gustave Eiffel agreed to help Bartholdi find a way to make Liberty strong. The system he devised was based on the principles used in his bridge designs.

Eiffel's brilliant design would give the colossal statue a skeleton of unusual strength and flexibility. The statue's main support would be a central tower made up of four vertical iron columns connected by horizontal and diagonal iron girders. Extending out from the tower in every direction would be hundreds of iron bars. The bars would be connected to steel "ribs" that would follow the shape of the statue's inner surface. The ribs would be attached to Liberty's copper skin in a special way, using brackets of copper that would act almost as springs. The design would allow Liberty to twist a bit in the wind. It would also allow the various metal parts

42

Eiffel is best remembered for his famous Eiffel Tower in Paris, which he designed for the 1889 World's Fair.

of the statue to expand and contract at different rates as the temperature changed.

Eiffel's design for Liberty's skeleton remains one of the most important engineering feats of recent history. The statue does not have to bear its own weight, since the copper skin actually hangs, like a curtain, from the iron supports inside. The methods Eiffel used in the Statue of Liberty are still used to build steel and glass skyscrapers, as well as airplane wings. Today, engineers call Eiffel's technique "stressed-skin" or "curtain-wall" construction. But his unique solution to the problem of supporting Liberty would not be his most famous accomplishment. Some years later, in 1883, he constructed the Eiffel Tower in Paris, probably the most famous tower in the world.

In the meantime, however, Eiffel had helped Bartholdi overcome a great problem. There were still others that had to be solved before Liberty could become a reality.

CONSTRUCTION IN PARIS

From the very beginning, Bartholdi had known that raising enough money to complete the statue would be a difficult task. A great deal of money was needed to pay for the copper and steel for the statue itself, as well as for the huge quantities of plaster needed for the scale models. The skilled workers who helped build the great work and shape the intricate copper sheets and central girders also had to be paid. Throughout most of the project, Bartholdi did not know where the money to build the final statue would be found.

Since 1875, when the Union Franco-Americaine had been organized, Professor Laboulaye and his associates had been trying to raise money for the project. But it was slow in coming. A special concert given in 1876 by the well-known French composer Charles Gounod raised only a small amount of money. Larger gifts were presented by some French towns, businesses, and citizens, but even by 1879 the fund raisers were still nowhere near their goal.

Finally, the committee held a great lottery offering more than five hundred prizes. Men, women, and even schoolchildren from all over France could contribute to the great gift for America and have a chance of winning a valuable prize as well. When the enormous lottery and a number of other fund-raising projects were completed, enough money to finish the statue had finally been collected. At a dinner held by the Union Franco-Americaine on July 7, 1881, it was announced that the Americans could expect the gift to be completed by 1883. With the money finally at hand, Bartholdi knew he could at last begin the final stages of construction.

The task proved to be a bit more complicated and time-consuming than Bartholdi had imagined. People who visited the

Bartholdi used a huge, high-ceilinged warehouse in Paris as his studio during the great project.

sculptor's studio in the early 1880s were amazed by what they saw. Clay and plaster models of the statue were placed throughout the cavernous room. Full-size fragments of the statue itself were situated all over the studio. Some of the pieces were enormous plaster molds, huge bits of a gigantic and confusing puzzle. Some of the molds were covered with an intricate network of wooden boards, while others were partially covered with large sheets of thin copper. Workmen seemed to be everywhere, hammering copper plates into shape, smoothing plaster surfaces, cutting thousands of pieces of wood, and always measuring and then measuring again.

Outside the enormous studio, the sight was just as strange. In the

Building such an enormous statue was a complicated process. After working on a series of smaller plaster models of the statue, skilled craftsmen built huge wooden frameworks and covered them with plaster to form full-scale models of each major section of the figure. These photographs show construction of the full-scale model of Liberty's left arm.

Next, carpenters built huge wooden forms (top) that followed the outer shape of the full-scale plaster models. Then, metalworkers placed thin sheets of copper on the forms and hammered them into shape (bottom). When the copper sheets were taken away from the wooden forms, their exterior surface matched the shape of the plaster model from which the wooden forms had been made. This ancient technique of shaping the exterior surface of metal sheets by hammering their undersurface is called repoussé forming. The hundreds of separate molded copper sheets produced by this process could then be hung together on the iron skeleton created by Eiffel.

In early 1883, while Bartholdi was busy working on the exterior part of the statue, Eiffel and his assistants began building Liberty's skeleton in a courtyard next to Bartholdi's workshop.

courtyard next to the large building, Gustave Eiffel and his workers were building the complicated iron skeleton that would support the statue. People who saw parts of Liberty scattered all over the inside and outside of the studio wondered if Bartholdi would ever be able to put them together.

By the early months of 1883, the great copper plates were ready to be attached to the steel skeleton. As the work progressed in the courtyard, a towering scaffold was built.

By spring of 1883, workmen were able to begin attaching the copper plates to the iron skeleton. Within a few months, the bottom half of the figure had taken shape (left). By fall, the statue was nearly complete (right).

Bartholdi, Eiffel, and their army of assistants had done their jobs well. With only relatively minor adjustments, all the intricate pieces fit together perfectly. It had taken seventeen years for the Statue of Liberty to evolve from Professor Laboulaye's suggestion to its present form, but from that point on the work went quickly.

By the summer of 1883, the unfinished statue was towering above the rooftops of Paris. Before the end of the year, the head and finally the right arm and torch were raised into position. The

Statue of Liberty—a dream now nearly two decades old—was at last a reality.

The French workers who built Liberty must have felt a tremendous amount of pride in their work. Before they presented the great statue to the American ambassador to France on July 4, 1884, the workers took down the intricate scaffolding so Liberty would look her best for the ceremony. Before the end of the year, they would have to put up the scaffold once more so that they could begin taking the statue apart, piece by piece, in order to make it ready for the voyage to America.

Some months earlier, however, Bartholdi had been amazed to discover that yet another great problem remained. After all the expensive and difficult work of nearly two decades, it suddenly appeared as if the Statue of Liberty would have no place to stand.

THE PEDESTAL PANIC

When Bartholdi had first proposed his great project, most Americans had welcomed the idea. But many also found it hard to believe that such an enormous statue could ever be built. After a writer for the *New York Times* saw the huge arm in Philadelphia, he wondered in print whether Bartholdi had given any thought to what would stand beneath the upstretched arm.

In 1877, while the statue was still in the planning stages, Congress voted to accept the gift and provide space for it on Bedloe's or another island in New York Harbor. Although most people knew that some sort of foundation would have to be built for the statue, five years passed before serious work on the pedestal began.

After considerable urging by Bartholdi, a famous American architect named Richard Morris Hunt finally began working on sketches for the pedestal. When Hunt completed his design, it was agreed that Bedloe's Island could be used as a site. The old star-shaped fort that had been built upon it could be repaired and used as a foundation for the pedestal.

Actual work on Liberty's pedestal did not begin until 1884, the year after the final statue was assembled in the courtyard outside Bartholdi's Paris studio. Then, before the base was even half finished, all work suddenly stopped. There was no money to complete the project.

Bartholdi was shocked to learn how far behind schedule construction of the pedestal had fallen. As the statue itself stood finished in Paris, the site for the pedestal on Bedloe's Island became nearly abandoned, and the star-shaped foundation was left covered with rubble and debris.

Members of Congress tried to introduce a law providing $100,000 to complete the project, but could not drum up enough votes to pass the bill. Many Americans, the congressmen learned, felt that the Statue of Liberty belonged to New York and therefore should be paid for by New Yorkers.

The statue had already been completed in Paris by the time serious work on the pedestal got underway. The foundation for the pedestal was made of 27,000 tons of concrete. At the time, it was the largest single concrete mass ever built.

BARTHOLDI.

Work on the pedestal came to a halt only a few months after it began because American fund raisers were unable to raise enough money to finish the project.

Without money to pay for workers or materials, no one was certain when, or even if, Liberty's pedestal would be finished. In Paris, Bartholdi became even more alarmed. In a desperate attempt to raise money to complete the pedestal, he rushed signed miniatures of the statue and other souvenirs to the United States, hoping they could be sold there.

Many Americans joined the struggle to raise money for the cause. A public speaker was hired to travel throughout the country and collect contributions. Special fund-raising sporting events, concerts, art auctions, and even a poetry contest helped to make citizens more aware of the plight of the great statue. The contest failed to raise money, but one of the poems written for it would eventually become famous. Some years later, Emma Lazarus's poem "The New Colossus" would be inscribed on the pedestal of the statue.

Despite the Americans' efforts, not nearly enough money was

collected to pay for the pedestal. By early 1885, when the completed statue was ready to be shipped to the United States, the pedestal stood unfinished on Bedloe's Island. Little more than half of the needed $300,000 had been collected, and public contributions had slowed to a trickle.

For the twenty-year dream of Laboulaye, Bartholdi, and so many others, this one great problem remained. Fittingly enough, the man most responsible for solving it was not a native-born American, but an immigrant who had settled in New York.

JOSEPH PULITZER

Like millions of others, Joseph Pulitzer had come to America hoping to escape a life of poverty in Europe. In 1864, after failing

Newspaper publisher Joseph Pulitzer launched an all-out campaign to raise money for completion of the statue's pedestal.

to find work as a soldier in his native Hungary, he traveled to America, where he fought for the Union army in the Civil War. After the war, he married and worked at various jobs until he had earned a substantial amount of money. In 1883, the same year that fund-raising efforts for Liberty's pedestal began to collapse, Pulitzer purchased *The World*, a New York City newspaper. When Pulitzer heard that work on the pedestal had been halted due to a lack of funds, he decided to take some action. Pulitzer was a clever man. He genuinely believed that a great statue symbolizing freedom was a worthy cause. But he also knew that he might be able to use the story to boost the circulation of his newspaper.

In May of 1883, *The World* ran an editorial attacking the wealthy citizens of New York. A single one of New York's many millionaires, Pulitzer pointed out, could easily donate all the money needed to complete the project. Pulitzer urged wealthy New Yorkers to make donations to the pedestal fund and asked other citizens to give whatever they could. But the campaign, though it brought in a little money, was not successful. By early 1885, the fund was still far from complete. Then, in March of 1885, only two months before the pieces of the statue were to arrive in New York Harbor, *The World* redoubled its efforts and launched an all-out campaign to raise the remaining money needed for the pedestal fund. Pulitzer promised to print the name of every person who donated to the fund, even if the contribution were only a nickel. To gain sympathy for the cause, he also printed messages such as this:

> Inclosed please find five cents as a poor office boy's mite toward the pedestal fund. As being loyal to the Stars and Stripes, I thought even five cents would be acceptable.

Pulitzer's tactics began to work. Soon, thousands of New Yorkers, rich businesspeople and poor schoolchildren alike, were donating money. Many of the donations were less than a dollar. Although the rival newspapers in New York City made fun of the campaign, newspapers in many other cities joined the effort to raise money.

The August 11, 1885 edition of The World *announced triumphantly that the pedestal fund's $100,000 goal had been reached. Pulitzer's campaign not only had raised enough money to assure completion of the statue's pedestal, but also had quadrupled the circulation of his newspaper.*

By August of 1885, five months after Pulitzer had renewed his campaign, 121,000 donors had given money to the pedestal fund. The $100,000 needed to finish the pedestal had finally been collected, and still the money kept coming in. At last, the foundation for the statue could be completed. The money had been raised none too soon. Liberty had already arrived in America.

Thousands of cheering spectators crowded onto the still-unfinished pedestal on Bedloe's Island to greet the French ship Isère, *which had carried the pieces of the statue across the Atlantic Ocean in 214 huge wooden crates.*

ALOFT IN NEW YORK HARBOR

On June 17, 1885, the three-masted sailing ship *Isère* arrived in New York Harbor carrying the disassembled statue in 214 wooden crates. Thousands of people were on hand to greet the gift from France. From the top of the still-unfinished pedestal on Bedloe's Island, a French flag was raised and people cheered as the ship made its way through the harbor. The many pieces of the great statue, hidden by their packing crates, were moved onto Bedloe's

Island to await the completion of the pedestal. With Pulitzer's *World* campaign in full swing, completion was now nearly certain. Workers hurried to finish the project.

For New Yorkers, the decade of the 1880s was an age of wonders. The Brooklyn Bridge had been completed only two years before Liberty arrived on American shores. More than a mile long, the wondrous 130-foot-high bridge carried people, horses, and wagons across the East River between Manhattan and Brooklyn. At the time the bridge was completed, its twin towers were the tallest man-made structures in America. But they would not hold the record for long.

With a newly built bridge, as well as many new tall buildings, New York City was fast becoming a land of giants. But on tiny Bedloe's Island, workers were busy constructing an actual giant. When she was finished, the workers knew, the Statue of Liberty would be the tallest man-made structure in the world.

During the warm months of 1885, stonemasons and laborers worked hard to complete Liberty's pedestal. In October, Bartholdi traveled to Bedloe's Island from France to oversee the work. He stayed only a month. There was nothing left for him to do. Once the pedestal was finished, all that would remain would be to put together the thousands of pieces of the giant puzzle. On hand were the 300,000 copper rivets needed to combine all the parts into one giant symbol of America.

The pedestal was finally completed in April of 1886. To honor the thousands who had contributed in small amounts to the pedestal fund, pennies, nickels, and dimes were mixed into the mortar used to lay the final stone. By summer, the statue itself was beginning to take shape. The huge iron skeleton designed by Eiffel was virtually complete. Day by day, new pieces of Liberty's copper skin were hoisted into position and riveted into place. New Yorkers were amazed by the size of the statue, which was easily visible from lower Manhattan. As Bartholdi's dream became a reality that was growing larger every day, local citizens could barely contain their enthusiasm.

On Bedloe's Island, workmen hurried to finish assembling the statue in time for the unveiling ceremony scheduled for October 28, 1886. By the end of September, only the head and torch were not yet in place.

Wealthy New Yorkers who had once been bored by efforts to raise money for the pedestal now desperately sought invitations to the unveiling ceremony. Scheduled for October 28, 1886, on Bedloe's Island, the great event would be headed by United States President Grover Cleveland, and Liberty's creator, Auguste Bartholdi.

But would Liberty be ready for her own party?

By the end of September, workers were still crawling along the scaffolding that had been built around the statue. Though most of Liberty had been completed, her head and torch were still not in place. Fascinated spectators could see the complicated iron girders that would support the thin sheets of copper forming the head and torch. Only a few weeks remained until the scheduled unveiling ceremony.

In October, workmen standing inside the head of the statue riveted into place the copper sheets forming Liberty's face.

The Statue of Liberty was ready in time. Bartholdi, Eiffel, and Hunt had done their jobs well. Except for some problems with the support for the statue's right arm, all the pieces of the intricate puzzle had fit together perfectly. Days before the ceremony, workers hurried to take down the scaffolding and put the finishing touches on the great statue. A huge French flag that was to be removed during the ceremony was wrapped around Liberty's face.

THE 1886 UNVEILING

The morning of October 28, 1886, was cloudy. A gentle rain began that would continue through much of the day. Nothing, however, could dampen the spirits of hundreds of thousands of New Yorkers who were ready for the greatest celebration the city had ever seen. A United States president and a French sculptor now famous throughout America were on hand to lead the festivities. Other French and American dignitaries had come to New York as well.

A great parade led crowds down Fifth Avenue to the southern tip of Manhattan, where ships were ready to carry all the invited guests to Bedloe's Island for the ceremony. Strangely enough, although the newest symbol of America was a statue of a woman, only two women were allowed to make the short voyage to Bedloe's Island.

The majority of the hundred thousand or so New Yorkers who, in small amounts, had contributed most of the money to build Liberty's pedestal were forced to watch the festivities from the Manhattan shoreline. Space on the tiny island out in the bay was limited. Those lucky enough to carry invitations to Bedloe's Island heard speech after speech delivered in the rain.

Bartholdi felt it was the happiest day of his life. His only regret, he said, was that his elderly mother had not been well enough to cross the Atlantic and attend the ceremony.

The New York and New Jersey shorelines were packed with spectators. The harbor was filled with boats of every description, many so crammed with excited passengers that they seemed about to sink. The crowds on Bedloe's Island awaited the magic moment when Bartholdi would be given the signal to drop the veil from the great statue's face.

The signal would not come. While Senator William Evarts was addressing the crowd, Bartholdi mistook a pause for the end of the speech and dropped the veil ahead of schedule. The rest of Evarts's speech would never be heard. As soon as the veil fell, his voice was drowned out by hundreds of blaring ships' horns, thousands of

This 1886 painting by Edward Moran captures the excitement surrounding the official unveiling of the statue on October 28, 1886.

cheering spectators, and a twenty-one gun salute. More salutes were fired from the many little forts around New York Harbor just as darkness began to fall.

In the growing darkness, Bartholdi beheld the great statue that he had dreamed about for so long. Perhaps it gave him a sense of satisfaction to realize that, in a way, he had been able to bring his

Bartholdi modeled the face of the Statue of Liberty after that of his beloved mother, Charlotte Bartholdi.

mother to the celebration after all. Despite the various sources the sculptor had used in creating his image of Liberty, her face was clearly that of Bartholdi's mother.

Because of the bad weather, the much-awaited finale of the celebration had to be postponed for four days. But on the evening of November 1, spectators, tugboats, and steamers once again filled the harbor. At seven o'clock, when daylight had faded away, workers lit Liberty's torch as dozens of skyrockets and Roman candles burst in the sky. Bartholdi was a bit disappointed by the torch. Although it was bright enough to be seen clearly, he had hoped that it would be much brighter—bright enough to light up the sky.

At the time, few people realized how brightly Liberty's torch would shine over the next hundred years.

For these immigrants waiting on the dock at Ellis Island, a new life was about to begin.

Chapter 4

Ellis Island: Gateway to America

From 1892 to 1932 more than twelve million people from all over the world traveled to tiny Ellis Island in New York Harbor. Hoping to find a new life in America, they left behind homelands in Europe, Asia, Africa, South America, the Middle East, India, and nearly every other spot on the globe.

These immigrants, and their children and grandchildren, helped to make America a great and prosperous nation. "More than a hundred million Americans had relatives who first saw America by sailing past the Statue of Liberty on their way to Ellis Island," said Lee Iacocca, first chairman of the Statue of Liberty-Ellis Island Centennial Commission.

For millions of immigrants, Ellis Island was the first crucial stop on the road to American citizenship. There, in clear sight of the Statue of Liberty, American officials determined who would be allowed to live in the United States and who would be turned away.

Most of the immigrants were permitted to stay and seek a better way of life in America. Only about 2 percent were forced to return to the homelands they had left behind. For the other 98 percent, the great adventure of life in America was about to begin. For them, as well as for their adopted nation, life would never again be quite the same. After the 1880s, more than ever before, America became the melting pot of the world. A great experiment had begun—one that is still going strong.

THE HUDDLED MASSES

"Give me your tired, your poor, your huddled masses yearning to breathe free," is the most famous phrase from the Emma Lazarus poem inscribed on the base of the Statue of Liberty. This description of the waves of immigrants who sailed to New York Harbor is an accurate one. The great majority of the immigrants were poor. For many, the price of a steamship ticket to the United States was enough to wipe out the savings of a lifetime. For large families, the cost was staggering.

Before the mid-nineteenth century, sailing ships were the only means of transportation for crossing the Atlantic. The trip from Europe to New York often took more than a month. Even after oceangoing steamships were introduced around the middle of the century, a voyage across the Atlantic lasted two weeks or more.

For those who could afford only the least expensive tickets, the long trip was spent in steerage, the dark and dirty space at the bottom of the ship. Often, hundreds of people were crowded into the cramped steerage quarters. One immigrant remembered, "We climbed down to steerage by going down a narrow, steep stairway. It was dark and slippery. Once there I saw people lying in bunks that were stacked up one on top of the other. The people did not have enough room to sit up in bed. The smell inside was terrible."

Night and day were indistinguishable in the poorly-lighted space, and passengers had to endure the constant odor of stale food and unwashed bodies. Toilet facilities were inadequate. Seasickness, caused by the rolling motion of the ship, kept some people in their bunks for days. Disease was a constant danger. Throughout the nineteenth century, about one in ten steerage passengers died during a voyage. Many steerage quarters were infested with rats that competed for the meager supplies of food.

For immigrants who had to travel in steerage, the journey to the United States was a harrowing experience. Steerage quarters were dirty, overcrowded, and poorly ventilated. During the 1800s, one in ten steerage passengers died during the trip.

Most immigrants tried to bring along enough food for the entire voyage. If a ship did serve food, it either cost too much or was unappetizing and poorly prepared. Often, dry bread and huge barrels of herring were the only foods provided by the ship for steerage passengers. One woman's strongest memory of steerage was the salty taste of the herring she ate day after day.

Even during the early years of the twentieth century, the trip to America from most parts of the world was harrowing. For those who could afford the price of a private cabin, the journey was much more pleasant. But for the vast majority of immigrants, the long trip meant weeks of misery and discomfort.

It is hard to imagine the joy most immigrants felt when they first sighted the American mainland. At last, the weary steerage passengers climbed out of their dark quarters and flooded onto the open deck. Edward Corsi, who came to America from Italy at the age of ten, recalled the moment when New York Harbor first came into view:

> Giuseppe and I held tightly to stepfather's hands, while Liberta and Helvetia clung to mother. Passengers all about us were crowding against the rail. Jabbered conversation, sharp cries, laughter and cheers — a steadily rising din filled the air. Mothers and fathers lifted up the babies so that they too could see, off to the left, the Statue of Liberty.
>
> I looked at that statue with a sense of bewilderment, half doubting its reality. Looming shadowy through the mist, it brought silence to the decks of the *Florida*. This symbol of America — this enormous expression of what we all had been taught was the inner meaning of this new country we were coming to — inspired awe in the hopeful immigrants. Many older persons among us, burdened with a thousand memories of what they were leaving behind, had been openly weeping ever since we entered the narrower waters on our final approach toward the unknown. . . .
>
> Directly in front of the *Florida*, half visible in the faintly-colored haze, rose a second and even greater challenge to the imagination.
>
> "Mountains!" I cried to Giuseppe. "Look at them!"
>
> "They're strange," he said, "why don't they have snow on them?" He was craning his neck and standing on tiptoe to stare at the New York skyline. Stepfather looked toward the skyscrapers, and, smiling, assured us that they were not mountains but buildings — "the highest buildings in the world."

FIRST STEPS IN AMERICA

When the ships at last were docked at piers along southern Manhattan, the newcomers were finally allowed to step onto American land. Carrying their meager possessions ashore, they then had to await the arrival of small boats operated by the United

States Immigration Service. The boats would carry them to Ellis Island, where immigration officials would decide whether or not to permit them to enter the United States. Frightening rumors would sweep through the crowds of immigrants even before they set foot on the island: America had suddenly closed her doors, and no one would be allowed entry! Immigrants must prove they had a large amount of money or they would be sent home!

Most of the rumors would prove to be unfounded. But by the time they carried their trunks and bundles of clothes onto the little boat heading for Ellis Island, many immigrants were in tears. Their fears about not having enough money were understandable. Most of those few travelers who had been able to afford a private cabin on the ocean steamer were not even sent to Ellis Island. Instead,

In this 1906 photograph, immigrants crowd the deck of a ship to get their first look at New York Harbor and the Statue of Liberty.

69

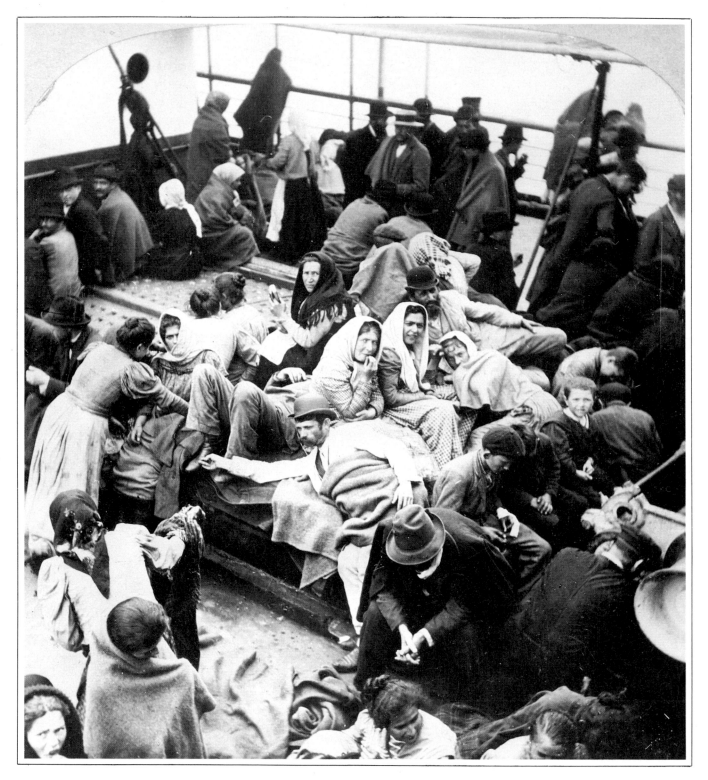

When the weather was good, steerage passengers were usually permitted to climb out of their cramped quarters to get some fresh air on the deck of the ship.

Ellis Island opened in 1892, when the federal government began handling immigrant processing. Seventy percent of the immigrants who came to the United States between 1892 and 1954 entered the country through Ellis Island. This 1910 photograph shows immigrants approaching the main building on the island.

immigration officials interviewed them aboard the docked ship. If everything were in order, they were allowed to enter New York City in a matter of hours.

All the steerage passengers, however, had to travel to Ellis Island. They must have been very worried about what was going to happen to them. There was always a chance that they would not be permitted to enter the United States. The steamship companies that carried immigrants to America had made an agreement with the United States government. If for any reason a person were refused entry into America, the company agreed to provide passage home, regardless of the immigrant's ability to pay. A sad journey home was a much dreaded possibility for the weary travelers to Ellis Island.

SWAMPED BY THE HUMAN TIDE

New arrivals were
given identification
tags, which were
pinned to their
clothing throughout
the examination
process. These Slavic
immigrants came to
Ellis Island in the
early 1900s.

During the peak years of American immigration, as many as five
thousand people a day passed through Ellis Island. For the officials
who tried to interview and care for the newly arrived immigrants,
the flood of humanity was often overwhelming.

Every time a new wave of people came off the Immigration
Service boat at Ellis Island, officials hurried into action. A large
identification number was pinned to the clothing of each
immigrant. Inside the main building, the immigrants were sent into
an enormous room, called the Great Hall, where they had to pass
through as many as twenty-two different inspection lines. The

After entering the main building (left), immigrants climbed a stairway to an enormous room called the Great Hall, where they were examined and questioned by immigration officials. When Ellis Island first opened, immigrants waiting their turn in the Great Hall had to pass through a maze of passageways made of iron railings. After 1911, these "pens" were replaced with long lines of wooden benches (below).

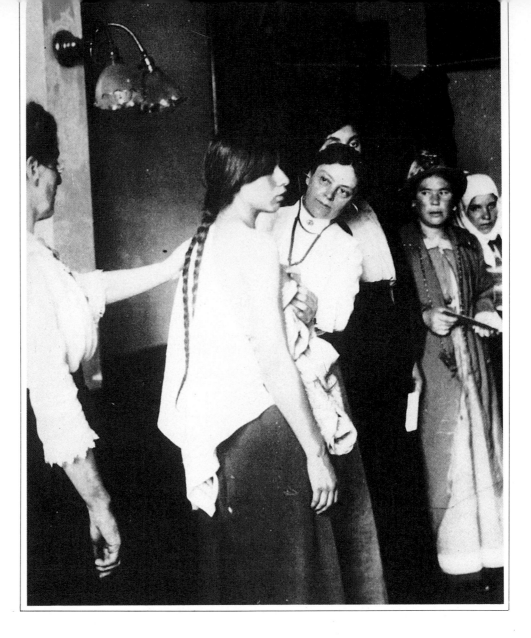

A doctor listens to the heart and lungs of a girl passing through Ellis Island during the early years of World War I.

experience must have been terribly frightening. At the head of each line was an immigration inspector, sometimes accompanied by interpreters, who would examine and question each person. A wrong answer — or improper papers — could lead to detainment or rejection.

United States Public Health Service doctors were the first to examine the new arrivals. Each immigrant was tested for a variety of illnesses and health problems. The doctors were called the "six-second" doctors by some people because they had to conduct their examinations so quickly. When a serious illness or some sort of deformity was suspected, the person's clothing was marked with

To test for trachoma, a serious eye disease, immigration inspectors had to flip a person's eyelids inside out. Many immigrants reported that this procedure was the most frightening part of their visit to Ellis Island.

chalk. A code was used to indicate the nature of the problem. K indicated hernia; L, lameness; H, heart trouble; B, back trouble; S, senility; and so on. An X was marked if a person was suspected of mental illness. It was not uncommon for an immigrant to have more than one chalk mark on his coat. If a person had an infectious disease, he was quarantined (sent for a period of time to a special room where he would be less likely to infect others).

A second team of doctors examined the eyes of each immigrant. Many immigrants, having heard terrible stories about this part of the examination, were terror-stricken as they approached these "eye men." In order to detect trachoma, an incurable and highly contagious eye disease, the doctors had to flip the eyelids inside out. The instrument used in those days was a glove buttonhook, and even though the procedure took only a few moments, it was a painful and frightening experience.

A medical examining room at Ellis Island as it appears today

Although the laws governing immigration changed over the years, some serious illnesses, such as trachoma, favus (a type of ringworm), and tuberculosis, were always cause for immediate rejection. Sometimes all but one member of a family would pass the medical inspection, and the others would, on the spot, have to make the agonizing decision of whether to stay in America or return with the rejected loved one. Fiorello La Guardia, who later became mayor of New York, worked as an interpreter at Ellis Island between 1910 and 1912. He described what it was like to witness such a scene:

> Sometimes, if it was a young child who suffered from trachoma, one of the parents had to return to the native country with the rejected member of the family. When they learned of their fate, they were stunned. They had never felt ill. They had never heard of the

word trachoma. They could see all right, and they had no homes to
return to. I suffered, because I felt so powerless to help these poor
people. . . . I never managed during the three years I worked there
to become callous to the mental anguish, the disappointment and
the despair I witnessed almost daily.

Immigrants who had diseases that automatically barred them
from entering the country had to stay at a special hospital on the
island until they could be deported. But those with less-serious
illnesses, such as measles or pneumonia, were treated at the main
hospital and then permitted to enter the United States.

Those who passed the health inspection then had to face a
barrage of other questions. The questions must have seemed
endless, the proper answers unclear. *Where were you born? What
is your birthdate? Are you married? Where did you last live? What
is your occupation? Have you ever been in prison or in a poorhouse?
Have you ever been in a hospital for the insane? Who paid for your
passage to the United States? Does that person live in the United
States? Where are you going to live in America? Who will you live
with? Is there someone to meet you here? Do you have twenty-five
dollars in cash?*

These questions, and dozens of others, had been carefully
prepared by the Immigration Service. With so many people seeking
a new home in America, a system was needed to find out quickly if
an individual had a good chance of surviving the first difficult
weeks in a new country.

In 1882, ten years before Ellis Island was opened as an
immigration station, Congress had enacted America's first national
immigration law. The law barred the immigration of the mentally
ill, the mentally disabled, criminals, prostitutes, and people likely
to rely on public welfare. Some of the questions asked by Ellis
Island officials were designed to identify such persons.

Surprisingly, one of the most problematic questions was the
very first one, "What is your name?" Quite often, the name an
immigrant had when he left Ellis Island was not the same one he
had when he arrived. Some immigrants wanted their names to

sound more American, and gave the officials shortened forms of their original names. But others had their names changed by busy or careless immigration inspectors who misunderstood names or spelled them as they sounded. It is said that once, when a German-speaking Jewish immigrant named Isaac was asked his name, he became nervous and replied "Vergessen" ("I forget"). The immigration official wrote down "Isaac Ferguson."

Some impatient officials purposely changed or "Americanized" names to get their job done more quickly. The Russian name Vladimir became Walter or Willie. Goldenburger became Goldberg; Skyzertski became Sanda. Most immigrants were afraid to protest the action of officials who seemed to have total control over their future.

After 1917, immigrants could not enter the country without passing a literacy test in either English or their own language. One eleven-year-old boy who desperately wanted to stay in America found a way to get his illiterate mother through the literacy test. He quickly memorized the passage she was supposed to read aloud, slipped underneath her long skirts, and whispered the words to her, so that she could repeat them to the official.

Some fortunate immigrants were able to pass all the tests and interviews in a single day. Before nightfall, they would once again be on a boat bound for a New York dock. From New York's Battery (the port district in New York City), they would travel to their new homes.

Having successfully completed all the necessary questions and examinations, these immigrants waited on the dock at Ellis Island for the ferry that would take them to New York City.

Immigrants waiting inside the main building at Ellis Island had this view of the Statue of Liberty.

But for many, some problem would arise during the battery of tests and questions. Even at the beginning of the twentieth century, New York was a huge and sometimes dangerous city. A few of its millions of inhabitants preyed on unsuspecting immigrants, ready to steal their meager belongings or take advantage of their ignorance of American customs.

Immigration officials tried to protect the new arrivals from problems they might encounter in New York. The very young and very old, those with very little money, those obviously weakened by the long ocean voyage, and women traveling alone were given special attention. Often, an overnight or even longer stay on Ellis Island was required.

DETENTION

Special problems caused hundreds of immigrants to be detained almost every evening. According to several immigration authorities who worked at Ellis Island during the early 1900s, a lack of money was one of the most frequent causes for detention.

Ellis Island officials refused to allow a penniless newcomer to leave the island. Instead, they sent telegrams to friends or relatives asking that money be sent or that someone come to the island to meet the detained person. Unaccompanied women, children, and older people also were detained until they were claimed by a relative. Because of the overcrowded conditions, and because both immigrants and their American relatives found immigration procedures difficult to understand, mix-ups occurred frequently. It was not unusual to find that a husband had been waiting *outside* the immigration office for a week, unaware that his wife could not be released from detention until he went *inside* to claim her.

The recreation room at Ellis Island, where immigrants who were temporarily detained on the island could visit with friends and relatives

In the Ellis Island dining hall, some immigrants encountered foods they had never tasted before, such as bananas and white bread. These immigrants are eating lunch, which was usually a thick soup or stew.

Providing adequate sleeping quarters and food for the army of detained immigrants was a constant problem. In the early days of the twentieth century, more than a thousand folding beds, stacked three high, were distributed throughout the sleeping quarters. But even these were not enough. On many evenings, immigrants had to sleep on benches, chairs, and even the floor.

Meals were served to those who were detained at the island, even if it were for only a few hours. Reactions to the food varied tremendously. Some immigrants thought it was delicious; others called it inedible. One Czech woman who arrived at Ellis Island in 1922 marveled at the huge meal she received: "The first meal we

got—fish and milk, big pitchers of milk and white bread, the first
time I saw white bread and butter. There was so much milk, and I
drank it because we didn't have enough milk in my country. And I
said, 'My God, we're going to have a good time here. We're going to
have plenty to eat!' " On the other hand, one official recalled that
at one point during the immigration center's early years,
immigrants were being given prune sandwiches for breakfast,
lunch, and dinner. Another official reported that kitchen workers
would serve cheese and meat that had been left out in the heat
overnight. In 1908, The United States Immigration Commissioner
took steps to improve the quality of the food. Still, during the
busiest years of immigration, it was necessary to serve as many as
nine thousand meals each day. Under these circumstances, it was
no wonder that some people found the food bland and
uninteresting.

*During the peak years
of immigration, the
kitchen at Ellis Island
had to prepare thousands
of meals every day.*

These Serbian Gypsies, who were rejected at Ellis Island and eventually deported, were probably among those who remembered Ellis Island as the "Island of Tears."

The majority of those held in detention eventually found a way to enter the United States. For them, the difficult journey to America and the frightening hours or days on Ellis Island finally came to an end. But, for various reasons, a small number of newcomers could not work out their problems. Eventually, they were deported. For them, Ellis Island would be remembered as the "Island of Tears."

THE BUSINESS OF IMMIGRATION

In the early days, all the major railroad companies had ticket offices on Ellis Island. In later years, the Trunk Line Association, which represented many different railroad lines, sold all the tickets. During the peak of immigration, between 1900 and 1914, railroad-ticket sales on the tiny island were phenomenal. On the busiest days, it was not uncommon for total ticket sales to approach $100,000. This is especially remarkable because in those days, a railroad coach ticket from New York to Chicago cost only $15.

Sometimes the railroad waiting rooms held enough people to

As they departed from Ellis Island, these immigrants were given copies of the Bible by members of the New York Bible Society.

This elderly Russian Jew was one of the millions of immigrants who passed through Ellis Island during its busiest years, between 1900 and 1914.

populate small cities. While waiting for tickets or boats to railroad terminals, pregnant women sometimes went into labor and had to be rushed to hospitals. Several people died, and a few others were murdered. As in every other phase of the operations at Ellis Island, language was a constant problem. One ticket agent supposedly learned to ask "Where are you going?" in almost every language but Chinese and Japanese, which he was never able to master.

Often, the ticket agent had difficulty understanding where the immigrant wanted to go. Some immigrants had a specific destination in mind but had trouble pronouncing the name. A German who said he wanted to go to "Linkinbra" actually meant Lincoln, Nebraska. "Deas Moyness Yova" turned out to be Des Moines, Iowa; "Pringvilliamas" was Springfield, Mass.; and "Neihork, Nugers" was Newark, New Jersey. After years of experience, many ticket agents became experts at solving these geographical puzzles. But if language was a problem on Ellis Island, it was even worse in New York City. Whenever possible, officials sent traveling immigrants to terminals in New Jersey, so they could avoid entirely the hustle and bustle of New York.

A second major business on Ellis Island was the money exchange. At the money changers' booths, the newcomers could exchange the currency of their homeland for American dollars or gold. The money exchange was a constant source of dispute. Few immigrants had any money to spare. If they felt they had been shortchanged, arguments could be fierce.

On the other hand, like everyone else at Ellis Island, the money changers and their assistants were greatly overworked. At times, the lines of immigrants in front of their booths seemed endless. Under such circumstances, it was easy for even an honest worker to make a mistake. Although immigration officials often listened to complaints from immigrants, cheating was rarely proved.

Considering the vast number of immigrants, the language barriers, and the problems of poverty, Ellis Island's service record seems remarkable. But the history of the immigration center was not without its share of major mishaps. Three events there, in fact, were among the great disasters of their day.

THE FIRE OF 1897

The original Ellis Island immigration station was a three-story building made of Georgia pine. The cost of constructing the building was about $500,000.

The original immigration-center buildings on Ellis Island were made of Georgia pine, a very fast-burning variety of wood. Shortly after midnight on the morning of June 15, 1897, a fire was discovered in some wooden sheds near the boat docks. It quickly spread to other buildings on the island.

New York Harbor police were immediately alerted. Within minutes, the little island was surrounded by fireboats and tugs that sprayed streams of ocean water at the burning buildings. The fire fighters' efforts barely slowed down the blaze. Soon, most of the buildings on the island were in flames.

Remarkably, on the night of the fire there were only about two hundred people detained overnight on the island. Often there were many, many more. Nevertheless, as the extent of the fire became clear, many of the immigrants began to panic. To restore order, the city rushed fifty police officers to the island.

Thanks to the hard work of police and firemen—and to considerable luck—not a single person on the island died in the fire. But the physical destruction was devastating. Virtually all the buildings, then valued at three-quarters of a million dollars, were destroyed. Worse yet, all United States Immigration Service records were destroyed, as well as the personal belongings of all the immigrants on the island. When interviewed later, every one of them claimed to have had more money than was required to enter the country. Since everything had been destroyed by the fire, officials could do nothing but accept their statements.

Some people were angry at the government for allowing such dangerous conditions to exist. *The World* offered this criticism: "If a private individual or corporation had put up huge buildings of inflammable pine on a little island in the bay, and had kept there as many as thirty-five hundred persons from all over the earth, public opinion would have risen in its might. But the U.S. government did it." Worse yet, at anchor only a few hundred yards from the island were several United States ammunition boats loaded with tons of gunpowder. Had the wind carried sparks to the ships, the disaster might have been much more horrible.

On a June night in 1897, a disastrous fire broke out on Ellis Island. Although all the buildings were destroyed, the two hundred immigrants who were detained on the island that night were quickly evacuated, and not a single life was lost. This photograph shows the island immediately after the fire.

The new immigration center opened on December 17, 1900. The main building, built of fireproof brick and limestone, was placed on the same site as the earlier building (right). Two additional islands, now joined into one island (left), were created to hold two hospitals, as well as a dormitory, restaurant, bathhouse, laundry, and other facilities.

Just sixteen days after the fire, Congress voted to provide $600,000 to rebuild the center. While the work was being done, the immigration station was moved to the Barge Office at Manhattan's southern tip.

It took more than two years to complete the work on Ellis Island. During that time, a huge brick and limestone building with hundred-foot-high towers was built. This building, as well as a number of others constructed soon after, still stands today. All are being cleaned and repaired as part of the Statue of Liberty-Ellis Island centennial.

In 1900, three years after the fire, a second island next to the original Ellis Island was made by dumping huge quantities of earth and rock into the relatively shallow waters of New York Harbor. A large hospital and a new restaurant and bathhouse for immigrants were built on the island. A third island was added in 1913. In 1920, landfill was added between the second and third islands to combine them into one. By 1934, the area of the Ellis Island complex had been increased from its original three acres to more than twenty-seven acres.

TWO DISASTROUS EXPLOSIONS

In the early afternoon of February 1, 1911, workers moved a shipment of dynamite from an American cargo ship to railroad cars at a spot on the New Jersey shore about a thousand feet from the western edge of Ellis Island. The cause was never determined, but for some reason, the dynamite exploded, creating an earth-shattering blast.

Many ship and railroad workers were killed and several hundred were seriously injured. On the island, immigrants and officials were horrified to see dismembered arms and legs falling down about them. A few immigrants and workers on the island were injured by flying glass, and an entire wall of the administration building was blown in. No one on the island was killed, but in southern Manhattan more than two hundred buildings were damaged.

An even greater disaster occurred about five years later, while World War I was raging in Europe. In the early morning hours of July 30, 1916, workers loaded ammunition to be used in the war onto a Russian ship docked at the mouth of the Black Tom River in New Jersey. At about 2:00 A.M., a German spy exploded dynamite that was on a barge bound for the Russian ship. Over a period of several hours, thirteen other barges loaded with gunpowder and munitions exploded.

The damage on Manhattan was incredible. Most of the windows in every building between the Battery and Fourteenth Street were blown out. Shock waves were felt even in the northern portions of Manhattan Island. But on Ellis Island, only a few hundred yards from the barges, the danger was even greater.

The wind was blowing from the west—from the mouth of the Black Tom River where the barges were moored—directly toward

Ellis Island. Raging fires lit the night sky. Soon, the thick ropes tethering the flaming barges to the New Jersey shore caught fire. As the fire burned through the ropes, a number of blazing barges loaded with shells and other explosives began drifting toward Ellis Island. Island officials rushed to move those in the hospital buildings nearest the approaching barges into the relative safety of open ground. As the boats exploded, shells shot into the sky like fireworks.

Before long, the situation became even more serious. The wind pushed several of the burning barges up against the seawalls of Ellis Island. Just when it looked as if hundreds of people on the island would be killed, several tugboats operated by the Lehigh Valley Railroad managed to pull the barges into the middle of the harbor, where they exploded relatively harmlessly.

For the rest of the night, the New York City Fire Department worked desperately to put out the dozens of fires that had started all over Ellis Island. Remarkably, once again not a single person on Ellis Island had been killed.

THE END OF AN ERA

By the time the Statue of Liberty was dedicated in 1886, there was already a growing feeling that America's open policy toward immigration could not last forever. In 1890, just four years later, the superintendent of the census announced that there was no longer an American frontier. With frontier land gone, where would the immigrants go?

Even after 1890, however, many millions of immigrants continued to travel to America. But as the years passed, ways were found to cut down on their numbers. In 1903, a law was passed barring the immigration of anyone with radical political opinions, such as anarchists (those who believe in having no government). During the years from 1907 to 1913, several laws were passed that severely limited the number of Asian immigrants. Despite these attempts at restriction, immigrants continued to pour into the

country by the millions. The peak years at Ellis Island, in fact, were from 1903 to 1915. The numbers began to drop only with the outbreak of World War I.

In 1917, immigration was further restricted by a law requiring immigrants to pass a literacy test. Anyone who could not read forty words in any language was to be rejected. This law was aimed mainly at people from southern and central Europe, where illiteracy rates were as high as 50 to 70 percent. In 1924, the National Origins Act was passed. The act set strict ceilings on the number of immigrants who could be admitted to the United States. During the Great Depression of the 1930s, immigration was restricted even further.

But immigration was not stopped entirely. Immediately after World War II, large numbers of Poles, Germans, Russians, Latvians, Yugoslavians, Puerto Ricans, and the European and Asian wives of American servicemen were allowed entry. Since the

Immigrants came to America from all over the world. These women arrived at Ellis Island in 1911 from Guadalupe, French West Indies.

After World War II, the United States experienced a wave of immigrants from war-torn European countries. This ten-year-old Polish girl was sent to America to live with her uncle.

1950s, the United States has accepted large numbers of refugees from such politically unstable countries as Hungary, Cuba, Vietnam, and Cambodia.

In recent years, however, the numbers have not been as great as they once were. Many of America's more recent immigrants, especially those from Mexico, chose to enter the country through California and Texas instead of through New York. Others began to arrive by plane rather than by ship. Although as many as a million immigrants a year once passed through its doors, Ellis Island gradually grew less crowded. The government stopped using it as an immigration reception center in 1932. The island continued to be used as a detention center, however, until it was shut down completely in 1954. For a number of years afterward, its buildings were allowed to decay. Then, in 1965, Ellis Island became part of the Statue of Liberty National Monument operated by the National Park Service. Although budgets were severely limited, some improvements were made on the island, and it was reopened for tourists in 1976.

From 1954, when the immigration center closed, until 1984, when restoration began, the facilities on Ellis Island were permitted to deteriorate. The ferry boat Ellis Island, *which had logged more than one million nautical miles shuttling immigrants between Ellis Island and New York City, was tied to its moorings and allowed to rot (top). The Great Hall inside the main building (bottom), where as many as five thousand immigrants a day were once examined, stood deserted.*

Chapter 5

One Hundred Years of Liberty

The Statue of Liberty stood in New York Harbor as every one of over twelve million immigrants traveled to Ellis Island in search of a new home in America. To millions, she was the "Mother of Exiles," a role originally assigned to her by Emma Lazarus in her 1883 poem "The New Colossus." Twenty years after the poem was written, when Ellis Island was at its busiest, the poem was inscribed on a bronze plaque and attached to Liberty's base.

From the beginning, the Statue of Liberty was meant to be a symbol of liberty and freedom. Before long, it also became a symbol of hope to millions of immigrants. But for nearly the first half century of the statue's existence, the United States government seemed uncertain about how to treat it.

For her first sixteen years, Liberty was officially regarded as a lighthouse under the control of the United States Lighthouse Board. However, although the statue quickly became a popular tourist attraction, it was not a very useful lighthouse. The electric lights installed inside the flame of the torch were too dim to be seen clearly by passing ships.

The Statue of Liberty during restoration in the 1980s

In 1902, the United States War Department, which had originally controlled the fort on Bedloe's Island, took over the responsibility of caring for Liberty. During World War I, as a gesture of hope for the millions fighting in Europe, Liberty's lighting system was greatly intensified. Powerful floodlights were installed at the base of the statue. Hundreds of windows mounted with shards of cathedral glass were cut into the torch, and high-intensity lamps were installed inside.

Almost from the outset, the Statue of Liberty has been one of the most popular tourist attractions in the United States. In times of peace and times of war, millions of visitors have flocked to the little island on which she stands. In 1924, the statue became a national monument, and in 1933, it became part of America's national park system, under the care of the National Park Service. After nearly half a century, Liberty had the recognition she deserved. She was neither a lighthouse nor a part of the War Department. Liberty was, and remains, a national treasure.

In the 1950s, a group of American citizens formed a committee to develop a museum at the base of Liberty's pedestal. The museum showed some of the many contributions immigrants had made to America. It was a fitting location for a museum devoted to immigrants. Over the years, Liberty had helped millions of immigrants find their way to America's shores. But soon enough, it would beome clear that the Statue of Liberty herself needed help. The help would come, not surprisingly, from the sons and daughters of many of those who had come to America as immigrants. It would also come from the citizens of France.

THE RAVAGES OF TIME

Over the years, various parts of the copper-and-iron statue became damaged by the salty air and pollutants of New York Harbor. The torch was the most badly damaged section. The windows that had been added to the flame in 1916 made the torch more attractive, but they also leaked. Rainwater seeped into the

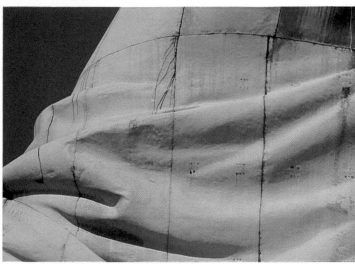

*The damaging effects of water seepage were evident in
the flame of the old torch (above) and in a section of
the iron ribbing near the cheek area (bottom right).
Rust stains appeared on various parts of the statue's
exterior, including this portion of the gown (top right).*

torch and arm and rusted the iron supports that held them up. By
the 1950s, the torch had become so weak that visitors were no
longer permitted to climb up to it. By the 1970s, the torch was in
danger of falling off.

In addition, thousands of the riblike iron supports that attached
the skeleton to the copper skin were badly rusted and needed to be
replaced. These were the most serious problems, but there were
others as well. In some places, the copper skin was badly stained
with rust. Also, about two square feet of copper had been eaten
through by corrosion and acid rain.

The inner surface of Liberty's skin, including this section inside her head (left), needed to be cleaned of dirt, graffiti, and old layers of paint. An adjustment needed to be made on Liberty's head, because it had become slightly tilted to the right and the crown was threatening to punch a hole in her arm (right).

The long-range effects of gravity also had made slight changes in the statue. Liberty's head had become tilted to the right. By the late 1970s, one of the points of her crown was rubbing against the uplifted right arm and was threatening to punch a hole in the copper skin. Because the iron skeleton had gradually settled over the years, some of the wires that kept the entire apparatus rigid had lost their tension. Finally, the stairs inside the statue had become slightly weakened, and the interior surface of the statue was, in some places, covered with stains and even graffiti.

Surprisingly, one of the statue's most serious problems had been caused while it was being built in 1886. During the final phases of construction, workers attached the head and right arm about two

100

feet to the right of where they were supposed to be attached. No one is certain why the workers did not follow Eiffel's plan for the arm support. Some people have suggested that the last-minute change was made because some of the copper plates for Liberty's right shoulder had been flattened a little during their trip across the Atlantic.

Whatever the reason for the mistake, the supports for Liberty's right arm were never as strong as Eiffel had intended them to be. Over the years, the inside of Liberty's right shoulder required a number of repairs. By the early 1980s, it was clear that another major repair was needed.

Help would come. The way it arrived made it seem as if history were repeating itself.

A SUGGESTION FROM FRANCE

In 1980, a French engineer named Jacques Moutard was busy repairing an old statue on Mount Auxois in France. Although the statue was much smaller than Liberty, it, too, had a copper skin over an iron skeleton. Moutard was surprised to find that the French statue was in poor condition. Knowing that the Statue of Liberty had been constructed in much the same way as the statue he was repairing, he began to wonder if it, too, were in need of repair.

A wealthy French philanthropist named Philippe Vallery-Radot was helping to pay for the repair of the smaller iron-and-copper statue. Moutard and Vallery-Radot discovered that similar problems had recently been uncovered in the Statue of Liberty.

The two Frenchmen realized that in only a few years, people in America and France would be celebrating Liberty's hundredth birthday. They had a magnificent idea. More than a hundred years earlier, two Frenchmen, Bartholdi and Laboulaye, had suggested creating the wonderful gift to America. Because of their hard work and the efforts of many others, the statue had become a reality. Wouldn't it be wonderful if the French people could help ready

Liberty for her hundredth birthday? The way to do that, of course, was to repair the damage she had sustained during her first century.

Philippe Vallery-Radot lost little time in developing a plan to help repair the great statue. Early in 1981, he began a series of discussions with officials from the United States National Park Service, the agency responsible for maintaining the statue. Soon, the French-American Committee for Restoration of the Statue of Liberty was formed.

Jacques Moutard and another French engineer, Philippe Grandjean, traveled to New York Harbor to study the condition of the statue. Before the end of 1981, other French engineers were also studying the statue's problems. Soon, a team of American experts headed by New York architect Richard Hayden was working with the French engineers to devise a plan to repair the Statue of Liberty.

Almost immediately, the experts realized they were faced with an enormous job. All the original designs for the Statue of Liberty had been lost. For reference purposes, new drawings that accurately showed every one of Liberty's thousands of parts would have to be made. Hours of careful examination of the statue resulted in a list of repairs that seemed endless.

By early 1982, the American and French engineers had completed much of their research. Most of the actual work lay ahead. But who would pay for such an enormous project? The French-American restoration committee organized by Philippe Vallery-Radot and the American National Park Service had managed to raise $5 million. But most of that money had been spent in merely studying the statue and deciding on the necessary repairs. As much as $30 million more would be needed. For the second time in a century, Liberty was in dire need of money.

A NATION COMES TO THE RESCUE

In May of 1982, President Ronald Reagan announced the creation of the Statue of Liberty-Ellis Island Centennial

Commission. Because the histories of the Statue of Liberty and the Ellis Island immigration center were closely tied, the American president decided to celebrate the hundredth anniversary of each by creating a single committee devoted to raising the money needed to repair both sites.

It was estimated that about $230 million would be needed to fund the project. The Ellis Island immigration center would not celebrate its hundredth anniversary until 1992. There would be almost a decade to raise the nearly $200 million needed for its restoration. But Liberty would be one hundred years old in 1986, only four years away. Approximately $30 million had to be raised relatively quickly.

Obviously, the drive for funds would need some high-powered direction. Lee Iacocca, chairman of the Chrysler Corporation and himself the son of an immigrant who had entered America through Ellis Island, was selected to be chairman of the Statue of Liberty-Ellis Island Foundation. Before long, advertisements asking people to contribute to the foundation began to appear on radio and television, and in newspapers and magazines. Almost a hundred years earlier, money for the Statue of Liberty's pedestal had been raised, slowly but surely, from businesses, private citizens, and schoolchildren. The new funds would be raised from the same sources. Before long, money began to trickle in.

By early 1984, the statue's appearance had begun to change dramatically. An enormous, 305-foot-high scaffold was built from the foundation of the pedestal to the top of the statue. With great

A bird's-eye view of the statue during restoration

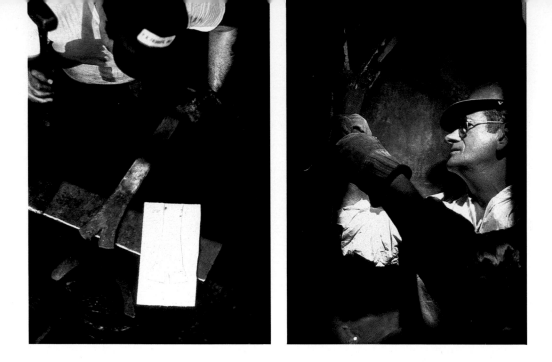

The iron ribs joining the copper skin to the supporting skeleton were removed and replaced. Following sketches of the original ribs, workers shaped new ribs out of stainless steel (left) and then riveted them into place (right).

care, the repairs began. Almost all of the eighteen hundred pieces of iron ribbing—every single one of them different—had to be removed and replaced with stainless-steel replicas. To avoid dangerously weakening the statue's supports, only four of the bars could be removed at one time. The weak right shoulder supports had to be rebuilt entirely.

All loose or missing rivets were replaced. Old paint was removed from the inner surface of the skin. Then the inner surface was cleaned, and small holes were carefully patched. The handrail on the spiral staircase leading to the crown was replaced and many of the steps were repaired. A number of areas around the windows in the crown also needed special attention. One of the points of the crown had to be carefully nudged away from the right arm.

The engineers decided to give Liberty an entirely new torch. The old torch was carefully removed. Then workers used Bartholdi's original method of construction to fashion a new torch that almost exactly duplicates the original. The new flame, however, has no windows and is covered with gold leaf. Instead of being lighted from within, it is lighted from the outside by sixteen powerful floodlights located around the torch's rim.

Several modern improvements were added to the statue as well. Before the restoration, on days when the hot summer sun beat down on the copper statue, people climbed Liberty's staircase in

temperatures of well over 100 degrees Fahrenheit. With so many people inside the closed statue, levels of carbon dioxide often became dangerously high. A new air-conditioning system, as well as improved rest areas along the stairway, were added to make summer visits to the statue much more enjoyable. A new, two-level elevator was installed to carry visitors to the top of the pedestal, making the statue more accessible to the handicapped. An emergency and maintenance elevator running from the museum level to the shoulder area of the statue was added as well.

The excitement and activity surrounding Liberty's reconstruction in the 1980s resembled that of the statue's assembly in 1886. The tools used for the project, however, differed greatly from those used when Liberty was constructed.

Modern chemicals and even liquified ultra-cold gases were used to clean the thin copper skin. Helicopters were used to remove the torch and a few other pieces of the statue. Walkie-talkies enabled workmen inside the statue to communicate with workers outside.

The engineers decided to replace Liberty's torch. First, the old, leaky torch was dismantled and removed (left). Then, using the original repoussé method of construction, French metalworkers built a new torch that almost exactly duplicated the original (right).

Technicians used liquid nitrogen and other abrasives to clean the inside of Liberty's copper skin (top left). Workers replaced the copper "saddles" that connect the skin to the stainless-steel ribs (bottom left). In November 1985, the new torch was lifted into place (right).

And modern, computerized equipment transmitted pictures and diagrams between offices in New York and Paris.

Throughout 1984 and 1985, work on the statue continued. By the end of 1985, much of the major work had been completed. In November, the new torch was lifted into place. Soon, the complex scaffolding began to be dismantled. Everyone involved in Liberty's restoration hurried to make her ready for her birthday celebration, which was planned for the 1986 Fourth-of-July weekend.

On July 3, 1986, a replica of the Liberty Bell was rung in New York City to signal the start of one of the most exciting birthday parties the world has ever seen. About eleven million people traveled to New York to witness the festivities, which began as a fleet of thirty-four naval vessels from thirteen nations sailed into New York Harbor and past the Statue of Liberty. On the same

On the first day of the celebration, some twenty thousand boats of every size and description converged on New York Harbor (left). That evening, French President François Mitterrand was among the speakers at the opening-night ceremony held on Governor's Island (right).

evening, retiring Chief Justice Warren Burger gave the oath of citizenship to fifteen hundred immigrants gathered on Ellis Island, while thousands of other new citizens were sworn in at other locations throughout the country.

On nearby Governor's Island, three thousand invited guests heard speeches by French President François Mitterrand and American President Ronald Reagan. Then President Reagan pushed a button that sent a mile-long laser beam to relight the torch of the famous statue. Millions of Americans watched the historic event broadcast live on television.

On July 4, spectators at New York Harbor
(left) watched Operation Sail '86 (bottom),
a magnificent parade of twenty-two tall
ships from all over the world. Even some of
Manhattan's buildings (top) were decorated
as part of Liberty's birthday celebration.

The following day, July 4, Operation Sail '86 got underway as twenty-two tall ships from eighteen countries paraded up and down Upper New York Bay. The major event of the evening was a spectacular fireworks show that lit up the entire southern half of Manhattan.

After being closed for more than a year, the Statue of Liberty was reopened to the public on July 5. On July 6, a cast of fifteen thousand performers, including many movie and pop-music celebrities, concluded the four-day festival with a flashy closing ceremony at Giant's Stadium in New Jersey.

For a century, the Statue of Liberty has held high a beacon showing the world the way to liberty. Now, this symbol of freedom is stronger than ever. It is up to us to see that the symbol remains a reality.

A dazzling fireworks display lit up the sky around New York Harbor on the night of July 4.

The closing ceremony at Giant's Stadium in New Jersey on July 6 featured spectacular special effects (top) and some fifteen thousand performers (bottom).

INDEX

Page numbers that appear in boldface type indicate illustrations.

ABOUT THE AUTHOR

JIM HARGROVE is a freelance writer who lives with his wife and teenage daughter in a small town in northern Illinois. He has written seven books for Childrens Press in addition to this one, and has contributed to works by more than thirty different publishers. As a child growing up in New York City during the 1950s, he climbed to the top of the Statue of Liberty more times than he can remember.

12 PEACHTREE

Hargrove, Jim.
  Gateway to freedom : the story of the
Statue of Liberty and Ellis Island /
Jim Hargrove. -- Chicago : Childrens
Press, c1986.
  111 p. : ill. (some col.) ; 27 cm.
  Includes index.
  Summary: Describes the designing of
the giant statue in New York Harbor,
the ideals of enlightenment and liberty
for which it stands, and the
immigration activities associated with
nearby Ellis Island.
  ISBN 0-516-03296-8

MAR 1 1 1988